FRENCH
for children

Catherine Bruzzone

Illustrations
Clare Beaton

PASSPORT BOOKS
NTC/Contemporary Publishing Group

Also available:
German for Children
Italian for Children
Spanish for Children
Inglés para niños
Each title in this series is a complete home learning course
with cassettes and a colorful children's Activity Book.

PRODUCED FOR PASSPORT BOOKS
BY B SMALL PUBLISHING

French-language consultants
Yolande Simpson and Nadine Monvoisin

Editor
Catherine Bruzzone

Design and Art Direction
Lone Morton

Typesetting
Lone Morton and Olivia Norton

Recordings
Gerald Ramshaw, Max II

Music
David Stoll

Lyrics
Catherine Bruzzone and David Stoll

Presenter
Nadine Monvoisin

Singers
Gertrude Thoma and Nicolas Mead

With special thanks to Nadine Monvoisin, her family and friends,
and Class 6e 5, Collège Jean Moulin, Chaville, France.

ISBN: 0-8442-9175-7

Contents

Learning French

Here are 10 simple suggestions to make learning French with Passport's *French for Children* much more fun:

 Learn with someone else if you can: perhaps a friend, your mom or dad, sister or brother. This course is full of games, so it's nice to have someone to play them with.

 Start with the cassette. Sophie will tell you what to do and when to use the book. Just remember to read Fun Facts and Superchat, and to fill in the Checklist.

 Listen for a short while, then go and do something else. But don't give up! When you listen again, you'll be amazed how much you remember.

 Rewind and fast-forward the cassette, and go over any section as often as you like.

 Say everything out loud – don't keep it to yourself. You could practice while you're taking a bath or out on your bike.

 Don't worry if you make mistakes. That's just part of learning a language.

 Sometimes an English word can help you remember the French: "chocolate" and **chocolat**, "six" and **six**, for example.

 Start a French scrapbook and put in everything you can discover about France – and all the other countries where French is spoken. There are at least 45 of them.

 If you're learning with a friend, give each other French names. There are some suggestions for names below.

 Enjoy yourself! It's a lot of fun speaking another language and one day it might be very useful too.

French names

Boys		*Girls*	
Alain	Marc	Madeleine	Dominique
Christian	Olivier	Marianne	Corinne
Claude	Pascal	Laure	Françoise
Patrick	Serge	Sylvie	Hélène
Julien	Yves	Cécile	Florence

1 Moi!

This is Sophie.
You'll hear her voice
on the tape.
She's going to help you
learn French.

Right from the start, you're going to learn:

- to say "hello"
- how to answer when someone asks you your name
- the numbers from 1 to 10
- how to answer when someone asks you how old you are.

Before you go on, listen to the tape.
Sophie will tell you what to do.
First, she's saying hello.
The words for the two songs you will hear are on page 69.

Naming names

Put an ✗ in the box when you hear the name.

☐ **Philippe** ☐ **Amandine** ☐ **Marc** ☐ **Laurie**

5

Put your name here!

bonjour
hello

comment t'appelles-tu?
what's your name?

je m'appelle _____
my name is

Fun Facts

There are at least 45 countries in the world where French is spoken! France, Canada, and Algeria are three. Can you discover some more?

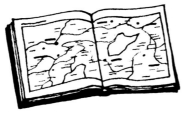

In most French-speaking countries, you shake hands when you meet people. If they are friends, you kiss them lightly on each cheek.

In French, when you say hello to a grown-up, you should add **monsieur** (sir) or **madame** (ma'am) to be more polite.

Comptons ensemble!

Listen to the tape.
Count these things with Sophie, and write the number
in the box.

How old am I?

Listen to the tape. Match up the names with the ages.
The first one has been done for you.

Hélène

Caroline

Croco

9   8   4   5   7   10

Annie

Alain

Eric

quel âge as-tu?
how old are you?

Put your age here!

j'ai ____ ans

I'm ____ (years old)

Salut!

Draw a picture of yourself here. Why not add a speech bubble with **Bonjour!** (hello!) or **Salut!** (hi!)?

Moi! Me!

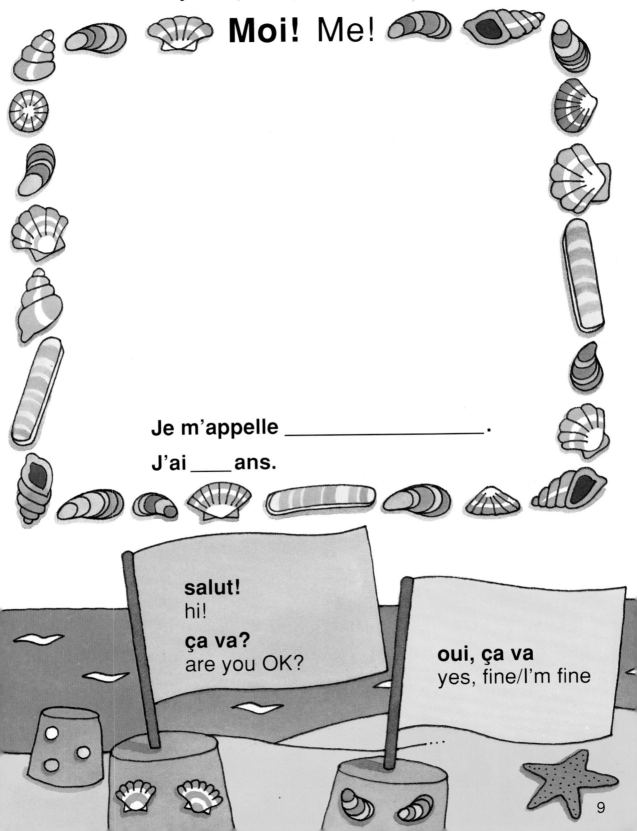

Je m'appelle _____.

J'ai ____ **ans.**

salut!
hi!

ça va?
are you OK?

oui, ça va
yes, fine/I'm fine

Checklist

Let's go over what you have learned in this unit. When you are sure you know what these mean, put a ✔ in the box.

- [ ] un   deux   trois   quatre   cinq   six   sept   huit   neuf   dix
- [ ] **bonjour! salut!**
- [ ] **je m'appelle** _____
- [ ] **comment t'appelles-tu?**
- [ ] **j'ai _____ ans**
- [ ] **quel âge as-tu?**
- [ ] **ça va? oui, ça va**

Try and say these out loud. If you have any trouble with them, why not listen to the tape again?

Super chat!

Bonjour, je m'appelle Superchat.

Un, deux, trois, quatre.

Salut, je m'appelle Monstrerat!

10

2 Marie et Paul

In this unit, you're going to learn:

- to say whether you like something or not
- to say "yes" and "no," and
- the names of some popular – and unpopular – things!

What are they saying?

First listen to the tape.
Now cut out the sentences below and paste them into the right bubbles. Now can you fill in the blanks?

J'ai ____ ans

Je m'appelle _____

Salut

J'ai ____ ans

Bonjour

Je m'appelle _____

I like . . .

Listen to the tape. Draw a line between **Oui** and the things you like and **Non** and the things you don't.

Oui ☺ Non ☹

The words for the song are on page 69.

j'aime . . . I like . . .
tu aimes? do you like?
oui yes
non no

Fun Facts

Stores you would enjoy going to in French-speaking countries.

Crêperie

For delicious pancakes, **crêpes**, filled with honey and different jams, or just sprinkled with sugar, as well as **galettes bretonnes**, pancakes made of brown flour called buckwheat.

les crêpes

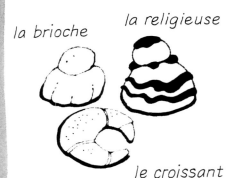

la brioche

la religieuse

le croissant

Pâtisserie

For freshly baked cakes like **croissants, brioches**, or **religieuses** which means "nuns" – can you see from the shape? This is filled with a special cream: **crème pâtissière**.

Librairie-Papeterie

For books, paper, colored pencils, felt-tip pens, scissors.

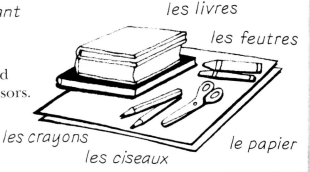

les livres

les feutres

les crayons

les ciseaux

le papier

Oui ou non?

Listen to the tape.
Marie and Paul's shopping trip.
If Marie or Paul say they like something, check the box next to the right picture below. Then cut those pictures out and paste them in the basket on page 15.

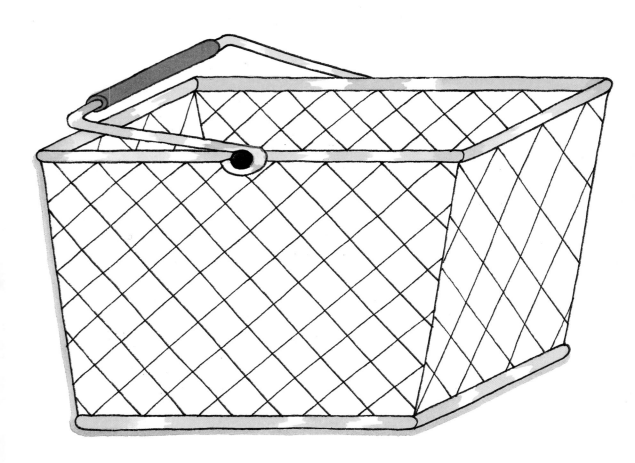

le Coca Coca-Cola
la limonade lemonade
le chocolat chocolate
le chat cat
la glace ice cream
la fraise strawberry
la pizza pizza
la sorcière witch
l'araignée spider
le monstre monster

Checklist

Let's go over what you have learned in this unit. When you are sure you know what these mean, put a ✔ in the box.

☐ **j'aime**

☐ **tu aimes?**

☐ **oui**

☐ **non**

☐ **le chocolat**   **le chat**
     le Coca   **l'araignée**
     la glace   **le monstre**
     la limonade   **la fraise**
     la pizza   **la sorcière**

Try and say these out loud. If you have any trouble with them, why not listen to the tape again?

Super chat!

J'aime le chocolat, la glace et la limonade.

BANQUE

Moi, j'aime l'or!

banque = bank
l'or = gold

Ouf! Une araignée!

3 À l'école

In this unit, you're going to learn:

- how to ask where something is
- how to say "goodbye" and "thank you"
- and some words about school.

Deal a number

This is a simple card game to practice
the numbers from 1 to 10.
You need a deck of cards and a die – and a partner.
You need only the 1 to 10 of hearts and the 1 to 10 of spades.
The ace counts as 1. Shuffle the hearts and deal out five cards each.
Shuffle the spades and lay them around in a clock shape, face down.
Decide who goes first.

1   *Player 1*: you throw the die and call out the number in French.
2   Then, move around the clock face that number of cards,
    counting out loud in French as you go. Use the die as a counter.
3   When you land, turn over the card and say the number it
    shows, out loud in French.
4   If the number matches a card in your hand, pick it up and lay
    down the pair. If not, turn it face down again.
5   *Player 2*: now you throw the die, call out the number, and move
    on around the clock just like Player 1.
6   The first player with all the pairs wins.

Now listen to the tape. First you will hear a song about
school. The words are at the back of the book on page 70.

Pierre's first day

Listen to the tape and point to the places and things around the picture. As you point say, **"là"** (there).

l'école the school

la salle de classe

les lavabos

la porte

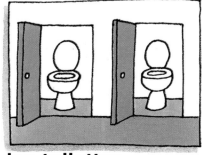

les toilettes

la cour

les copains

la maîtresse

où est? where is?
où sont? where are?
là there

19

Fun Facts

École primaire (elementary school)

In France, they go to the **école primaire** from age 6 to age 11

They start in the morning at

and finish at

They go to school on
Saturday morning . . .
but they have
Wednesday off.

They take their books in **un cartable à dos,** and
they have a lot of homework.
If they don't get good grades on their report
card at the end of the year, they have to stay in
the same class for one more year!

Guess the card

Play this game with a friend.
Make 9 cards: trace or copy the pictures around the edge of the
playground scene on pages 18 and 19. Shuffle them and lay them
out face down.
1   *Player 1:* will ask where something is. Use, **"où est?"** or
    "où sont?"
2   *Player 2:* points to a card and says, **"là."**
3   If the guess is right, *Player 2* wins a point.
4   The first player with 10 points wins.
    (Shuffle the cards between each try.)

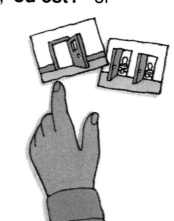

Now go on to the activity on page 21
before you go back to the tape.

Hidden pictures

There are three things hidden in this picture.
Can you find them? These questions will give you a clue.

Où est le chocolat?
Où est le chat?
Où sont les copains?

Then go back to the tape.

merci thank you
au revoir goodbye

Checklist

Let's go over what you have learned in this unit. When you are sure you know what these mean, put a ✔ in the box.

- [ ] **où est?**
- [ ] **où sont?**
- [ ] **là**
- [ ] **merci**
- [ ] **au revoir**
- [ ] **l'école**   **la porte**
  la maîtresse   **la cour**
  les copains   **les toilettes**
  la salle de classe   **le lavabo**

Try and say these out loud. If you have any trouble with them, why not listen to the tape again?

Super chat!

Je m'appelle Inspecteur Gros.

BANQUE

Oh non, la porte! Où est l'or?

Monstrerat est le voleur??

Où est Superchat?

Là.

inspecteur = inspector
gros = big, fat

le voleur = the thief

4 Ma famille

In this unit, you're going to learn:

- the names for "mom," "dad," "sister," and "brother"
- how you would be introduced to someone's family
- how to introduce your own family
- how to say how many brothers and sisters you have.

But first, listen to the tape and try the quiz. Then do the word puzzle below.

Puzzle

See if you can find these words hidden in the square. They're the same as the ones in the quiz, so you should know what they mean.

B	A	U	R	E	V	O	I	R	M
R	S	E	N	D	E	U	X	C	G
U	K	R	I	W	M	I	A	Y	A
D	U	V	T	H	N	B	D	A	Q
I	N	E	M	E	R	C	I	R	U
R	T	R	G	R	O	E	R	N	A
L	S	V	T	O	I	T	H	B	T
O	U	C	B	O	N	J	O	U	R
D	I	X	N	W	D	S	F	R	E
F	X	E	B	H	S	R	O	E	R

UN
QUATRE
AU REVOIR
DEUX
OUI
MERCI
BONJOUR
DIX

23

La famille Boomerang

Listen to the tape. You'll be meeting this kangaroo family.

ma sœur Florence

Maman

Papa

Julie   **mon frère Simon**   **ma sœur Élise**

The words for the song are on page 70.

voici	here is
la famille	family
papa	dad
maman	mom
ma sœur	my sister
mon frère	my brother

Fun Facts

In France, Christmas, **Noël**, is a family holiday. Everyone, even young children, stays up late on Christmas Eve for **le réveillon –** the main Christmas meal. Children put out shoes for their presents.

On Christmas Day, they also have a special lunch with turkey, a Christmas log, **une bûche de Noël**, and candied chestnuts, **marrons glacés**.

The exciting and colorful Carnival in New Orleans, USA, comes originally from France. It is held on a day called **Mardi Gras**, which means "Fat Tuesday" in French. Everyone dresses in costumes and dances in the streets.

j'ai __ frères	I've got __ brothers
j'ai __ sœurs	I've got __ sisters
je n'ai pas de frères	I don't have any brothers
je n'ai pas de sœurs	I don't have any sisters

Ma famille

Draw a picture of your own family.
Copy the labels below, so you can describe your picture in French. Then try the game on page 27.

| ma sœur | mon frère | Maman | Papa |

j'ai ___ sœurs   **j'ai ___ frères**

je n'ai pas de frères   **je n'ai pas de sœurs**

You may also need:
my grandma, **ma Mamie**, and my grandpa, **mon Papi**.

Voici ma famille

This is an "introducing game" for 2 players.
You need a die and two markers (buttons will do fine).
Decide who goes first.

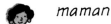 maman

 papa

 ma sœur

mon frère

1 *Player 1:* throw the die and move that number of spaces – count in French as you go!
2 When you land, introduce the person who appears on that square to *Player 2.* Say, **"voici . . ."**
3 *Player 2:* you reply, **"bonjour,"** and then it's your turn to throw the die.
4 The first player to reach the ice cream wins.

Checklist

Let's go over what you have learned in this unit. When you are sure you know what these mean, put a ✔ in the box.

☐ **voici**

☐ **maman**   **papa**

☐ **mon frère**   **ma sœur**

☐ **j'ai _____ frères**

☐ **j'ai _____ sœurs**

☐ **je n'ai pas de frères**

☐ **je n'ai pas de sœurs**

Try and say these out loud. If you have any trouble with them, why not listen to the tape again?

Super chat!

La famille de Monstrerat.

Voici papa!

J'ai cinq sacs d'or.

sacs = sacks
d'or = of gold

Merci, papa!

5 La maison

In this unit, you're going to learn:

- another answer to the question "where is?" **(où est?)**
- how to ask "what's that?" – very useful if you don't know the name of something in French!
- and how to give the answer
- to understand the word for "please"
- the names for rooms and furniture in the home.

Start with this game.
Listen to the tape before you read ahead.

Which hand?

You've probably played this game before. Now play it in French!
You'll need a partner. You're going to guess which
hand your partner's holding something in.
Find a pebble, **un galet.**

1 Now one of you will hold the pebble
  behind your back and ask your partner:
  "Où est le galet?"
2 Your partner must touch one of your
  arms and say **"là"** (there).
3 If it's right, he or she wins one point.
4 Then change places.
5 The first to get 10 points wins.

La maison d'une sorcière

Listen to the tape. You'll find out whose house this is.

la salle de bains

un lavabo

la porte

une table

un frigo

la cuisine

qu'est-ce que c'est? what's this?
c'est it's
ici here
s'il vous plaît please

la chambre

un lit

une chaise

une télé

le salon

Qu'est-ce que c'est?

You'll need a partner to play this game.
First cut out some small pieces of paper, this size:
and cover the pictures in the maze below.

1 *Player 1:* call out a number from 1 to 6 in French.
2 *Player 2:* start from that number and find the way to the picture.
3 Uncover it and ask, **"qu'est-ce que c'est?"**
4 *Player 1:* Give the answer, **"c'est un . . . "** or **"c'est une . . . "**
5 Then it's *Player 2's* turn to call a number.

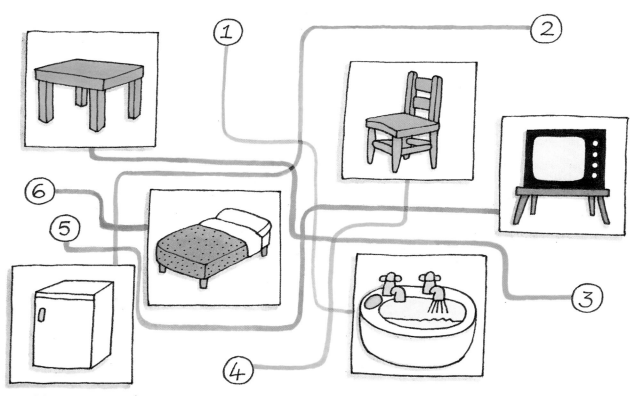

You could make new picture cards like these with some of the other
words you know and play the game again.

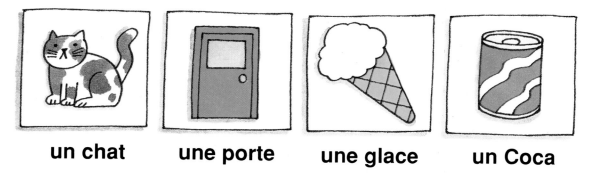

un chat   **une porte**   **une glace**   **un Coca**

Fun Facts

In big cities, most French-speaking people live in apartments, **appartements**. An apartment building is taken care of by a very important person called a **concierge**. He or she cleans the hallway, stairs, and elevator, **ascenseur**, waters the plants, sorts the mail, and keeps a look-out for unwanted visitors.

Houses often have wooden shutters, **volets**, that are closed at night.

Sometimes beds have a long, round pillow called **un traversin**.

Listen to the song on tape. You can join in with the words, which are on page 71 at the back of the book.

Checklist

Let's go over what you have learned in this unit. When you are sure you know what these mean, put a ✔ in the box.

- [ ] **qu'est-ce que c'est?**
- [ ] **c'est un/une . . .**
- [ ] **c'est ici**
- [ ] **s'il vous plaît**
- [ ] **la maison**
  la cuisine
  la salle de bains
  le salon
  la chambre

une table
un frigo
une chaise
une télé
un lit

Try and say these out loud. If you have any trouble with them, why not listen to the tape again?

la superauto = supercar

6 En voyage

In this unit, you're going to learn:

- to say what you like doing
- to say what you don't like doing
- to count up to 20.

Spot the differences

First, there are 5 differences between these two pictures.
Can you spot them? The answers are under Picture 1.
Next, can you name 8 things in Picture 1,
out loud in French?
You'll hear the answers on tape.

Label on bottle; picture; cakes on plate;
dials on TV; pattern on tablecloth.

En auto

Listen to the tape.
What does the Lefèvre family like to do in the car?

The words for the song are at the back of your book on page 71.

qu'est-ce que tu aimes faire? what do you like to do?
j'aime lire I like to read
j'aime écouter la radio I like to listen to the radio
j'aime manger I like to eat
j'aime chanter I like to sing
je n'aime pas manger I don't like to eat
je n'aime pas chanter I don't like to sing

Speeding and traffic jams

This is a game like *Chutes and Ladders* – you speed up the empty freeways and crawl back down into the traffic jams! You'll need a partner, two markers (buttons will do), and a die.
The first to get to the country in the last square wins.
If you land on any of these pictures, you must say, in French:

 I like to listen to the radio

 I don't like to listen to the radio

 I like to eat

 I like to sing

 I like to read

 I don't like to read

 I don't like to eat

 I don't like to sing

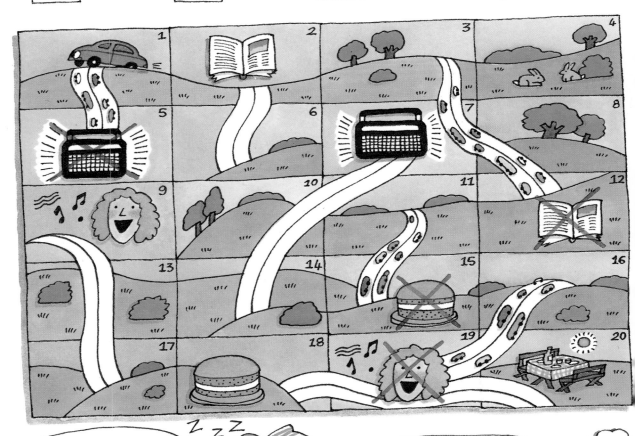

j'aime dormir

j'aime voyager

Can you guess what these two are saying?

Spin a number

You can play this game on your own or with a friend.
Make the spinner from a piece of cardboard. Trace or copy the
shape shown here. Push a pencil or stick through the center.
Twirl the spinner and say the number that it rests on, out loud in
French. Take turns if you are playing with a friend.

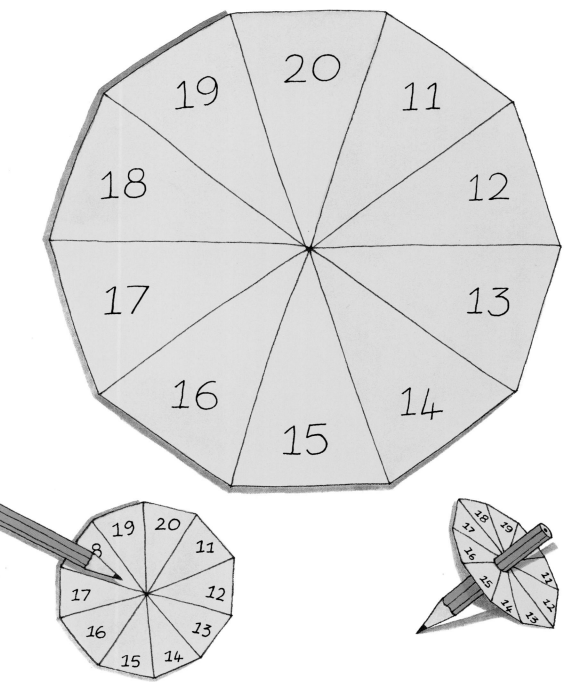

Fun Facts

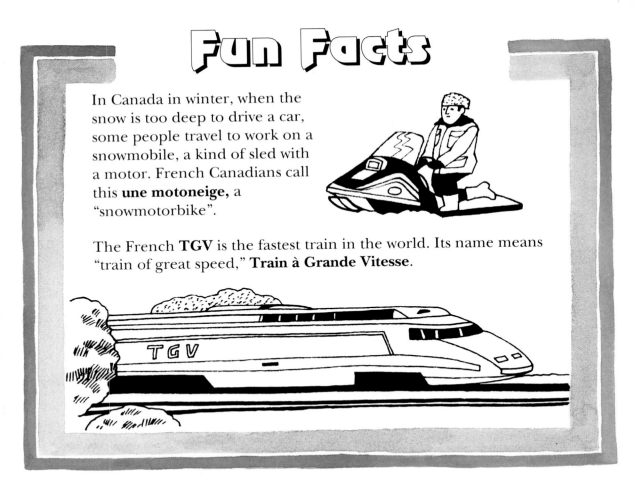

In Canada in winter, when the snow is too deep to drive a car, some people travel to work on a snowmobile, a kind of sled with a motor. French Canadians call this **une motoneige,** a "snowmotorbike".

The French **TGV** is the fastest train in the world. Its name means "train of great speed," **Train à Grande Vitesse**.

Bingo

Use a pencil to fill in this card with any numbers from 1 to 20. (If you don't press too hard, you can erase them and play again.) Then listen to the tape and cross out the numbers as they are called. Can you get your parents or a friend to play with you and call out different numbers?

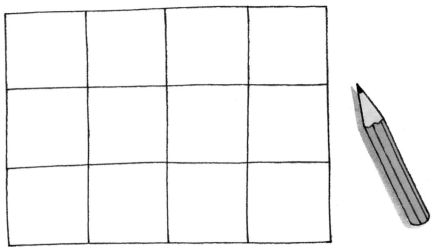

Checklist

Let's go over what you have learned in this unit. When you are sure you know what these mean, put a ✔ in the box.

onze	**douze**	**treize**	**quartorze**	**quinze**

seize   **dix-sept**   **dix-huit**   **dix-neuf**   **vingt**

☐ **qu'est-ce que tu aimes faire?**

☐ **j'aime chanter**
j'aime manger
j'aime écouter la radio

☐ **je n'aime pas voyager**
je n'aime pas lire
je n'aime pas dormir

Try and say these out loud. If you have any trouble with them, why not listen to the tape again?

Super chat!

J'aime écouter la radio...

...et j'aime chanter.

Je n'aime pas voyager!

7 Rouge et noir

In this unit, you're going to learn:

- the colors
- how to say "big" and "small"
- and to understand someone who is asking you what you want.

Listen to the tape before you go on. There's a song to start off with. The words are on page 72.

De quelle couleur?

Point to the colors as you hear them on tape.

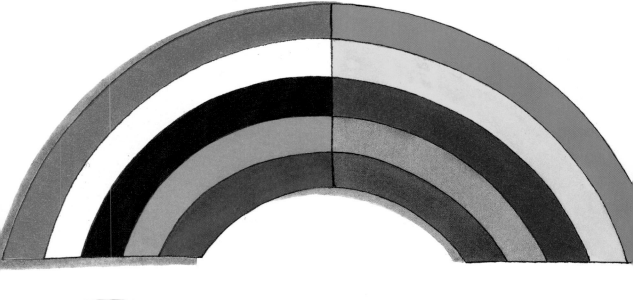

Racing colors

Who will reach the finish line first?
You can play with one or two partners – or even on your own.
Cut out the horses below, and decide who starts. You need a die.

1   *Player 1*: throw the die and move that number of squares along
    the track – counting in French, of course.
2   Each time, say the color of the square you land on in French.
3   If you can't remember it, or if it's wrong, go back two squares.
4   Then it's *Player 2's* turn to throw the die.

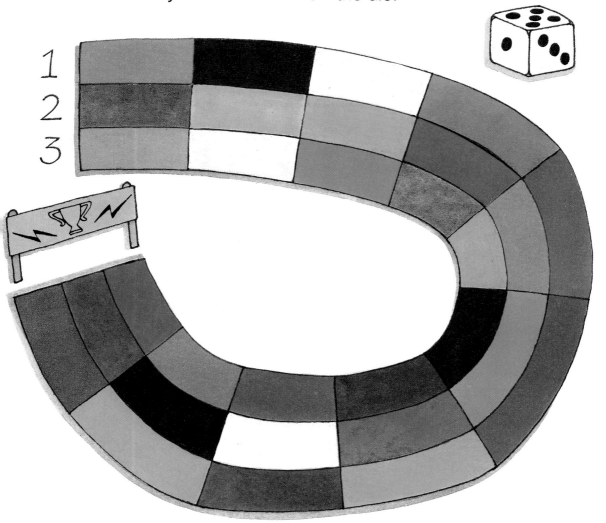

 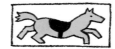 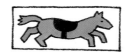

Match the colors

First make 10 cards to match the squares on the boards below, the same size and color. They can be paper or cardboard. Then put them in a box or mix them up on the floor, face down.
You'll need a partner to play this game.
Choose a board and decide who starts.

1 *Player 1:* will pick a card from the box and call out the color in French.
2 Whoever has that color on their board calls out, **"c'est à moi!"** (it's mine!).
3 They then take the card and place it on their board on the matching square.
4 Then it's *Player 2's* turn to pick a card.
5 The first to cover a board is the winner.

c'est à moi that's mine/it's mine
s'il te plaît please *(to friends and family)*

Les ballons

Listen to the tape.

le ballon   balloon
tu veux . . . ?   do you want . . . ?
gros   big
petit   small
voilà   here you are

Take your pick

Listen to the tape. Decide which balloon is being called and mark the correct box.

Fun Facts

Here are three flags of countries where French is spoken. Can you find out what colors they should be and color them in yourself?

La France   **Le Cameroun**   **Le Canada**

Checklist

Let's go over what you have learned in this unit. When you are sure you know what these mean, put a ✔ in the box.

☐ **bleu rouge noir blanc jaune**

gris vert violet marron orange

☐ **gros**

☐ **petit**

☐ **tu veux . . . ?**

☐ **voilà**

☐ **c'est à moi**

☐ **s'il te plaît**

Try and say these out loud. If you have any trouble with them, why not listen to the tape again?

¡Super chat!

À la fête foraine.

Le rouge!

Le bleu!

la fête foraine = amusement park

Au café.

Tu veux un Coca aussi?

au café = at the snack bar

CAFÉ

Voilà Monstrerat!

8 Le zoo

In this unit, you're going to learn:

- the names of some zoo animals
- how to say you're hungry, thirsty, or afraid
- how to ask for something in a snack bar or restaurant
- how to say that something's super, big, great, etc.

Listen to the tape before you go on.

Les animaux

Here are the animals you'll be meeting in this unit. Can you spot 5 differences between the two pictures?

la giraffe

l'éléphant

le lion

le singe

le dauphin

Do the activity on page 48 before you go back to the tape.

Giraffe/leaves; dolphin/mouth; elephant/tusks; monkey/tail; lion/ears.

Where are they?

Fit each animal below into its place in the picture above.

Can you write in the names of these animals in French?
Look back at page 47, if you need help.
Then go back to the tape.

Are they hungry or thirsty?

Listen to the tape.
These animals will say if they are hungry or thirsty.
Draw some food or a drink for them in the box next to each
animal. If you're not sure what they eat, just make it up.

J'ai peur!

qu'est-ce qu'il y a?
what's the matter?
j'ai faim I'm hungry
j'ai soif I'm thirsty
j'ai peur I'm afraid
moi aussi me too

Snick snack

Listen to the children ordering a snack at the zoo snack bar.
Draw a line to connect the food and drink each child orders.
The first one has been done for you.

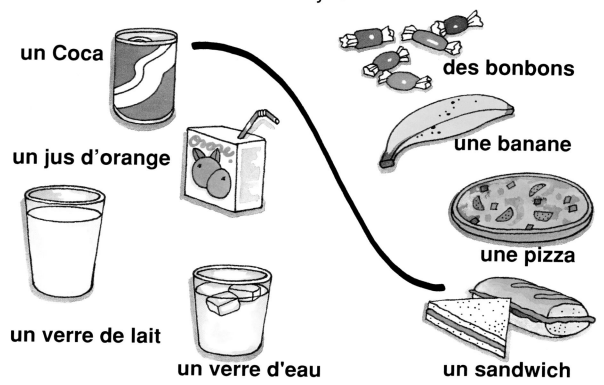

un Coca

des bonbons

un jus d'orange

une banane

une pizza

un verre de lait

un verre d'eau

un sandwich

Now trace or copy those pictures and play a game with a friend.
One person be the snack bar owner and the other ask for a drink and
a snack. Try to use all the language in the hamburger below.
You could also use pictures of other things you already know in
French: ice cream, strawberries, lemonade, and so on.

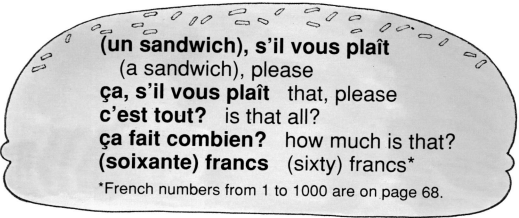

(un sandwich), s'il vous plaît
(a sandwich), please
ça, s'il vous plaît   that, please
c'est tout?   is that all?
ça fait combien?   how much is that?
(soixante) francs   (sixty) francs*
*French numbers from 1 to 1000 are on page 68.

Fun Facts

Just as all over the world, French-speaking children enjoy fun fairs, **fêtes foraines.**

On July 14, Bastille Day, every town and village in France is decorated with flags or colored lights, and you can go dancing in the streets! There are fun fairs, races, and fireworks displays.

Can you find out why French people celebrate Bastille Day?

c'est grand! it's big!
c'est chouette! it's super!
c'est amusant! it's fun!
c'est extra! it's great!
c'est bon! it's good! (of food)

The words for the song are at the back of the book on page 72.

Checklist

Let's go over what you have learned in this unit. When you are sure you know what these mean, put a ✔ in the box.

- [ ] **qu'est-ce qu'il y a?**

- [ ] **j'ai faim**   **j'ai soif**   **j'ai peur**

- [ ] **le lion**   **le dauphin**   **le singe**
  l'éléphant   **la girafe**

- [ ] **un jus d'orange**   **une banane**
  un verre de lait   **des bonbons**
  un verre d'eau   **un sandwich**

- [ ] **c'est grand!**   **c'est chouette!**   **c'est bon!**
  c'est amusant!   **c'est extra!**

- [ ] **ça, s'il vous plaît**   **ça fait combien?**   **c'est tout?**

9 Le pique-nique

In this unit, you're going to learn:

- how to talk about the weather
- how to answer if someone offers you "a little" food
- the names of some food in French.

First let's listen to the weather song on tape.
The words are on page 73.

What's the weather like today?

Listen to the tape and write an ✗ next to the right picture.

il fait chaud it's hot
il fait froid it's cold

il fait beau
the weather's fine
il pleut it's raining

Fun Facts

Good things to eat

France

There are at least 365 different cheeses in France – one for each day of the year!

Une baguette is the name for a loaf of French bread. Do you know what shape it is? You can see it on this page.

Le steak-frites, steak and french fries, is sometimes called the French national dish. It's not very unusual but very popular!

Algeria, Morocco, Tunisia

In these three French-speaking countries of North Africa, **couscous** is the most popular dish. It is made of grains of wheat called semolina and steamed in a special pot, called a **couscousier**. It is usually served with lamb and vegetable stew.

Canada

A favorite dish in Canada is **tourtière**, a big meat pie with lots of spices. It can stop a snowstorm in its tracks!

Yum, yum

Find the picture that matches the first one in each row.
Check the tape to hear how you say these foods in French.

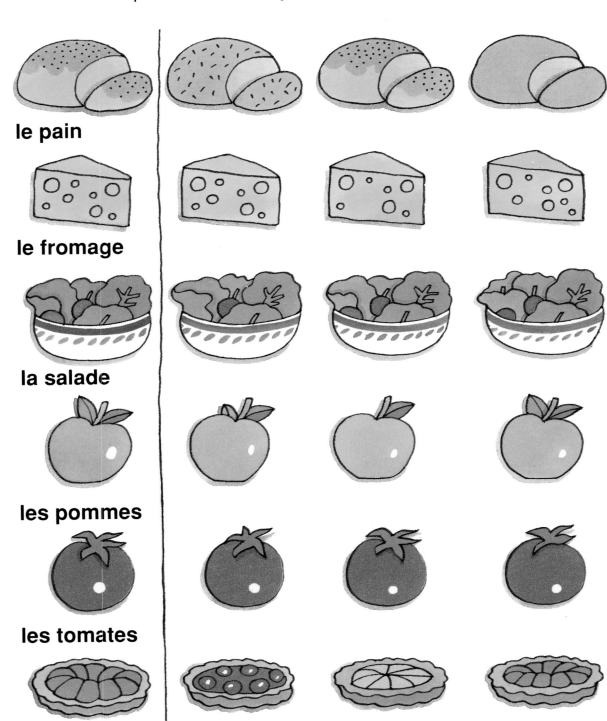

le pain

le fromage

la salade

les pommes

les tomates

les tartelettes

Au soleil

Listen to the conversation on tape.
Here is the picture it's describing.
Can you match the sentences below with the people in the
picture who are saying them?
Write the sentences in the speech bubbles, if you want.

Checklist

Let's go over what you have learned in this unit. When you are sure you know what these mean, put a ✔ in the box.

☐ **il fait beau**

☐ **il fait froid**

☐ **il fait chaud**

☐ **il pleut**

☐ **tu veux un peu de . . . ?**

☐ **le pain   la salade**
le fromage   la tomate
la pomme   la tartelette

☐ **bon appétit!   merci**

Try and say these out loud. If you have any trouble with them, why not listen to the tape again?

Oh non, il pleut!

Super chat!

C'est fini!

fini = finished

Il fait froid.

58

10 Joyeux anniversaire!

In this unit, you're going to learn:

- how to say that you'd like something
- how to say the names of some popular toys
- and you'll go over some of the language you've learned before.

Before you start, listen to the tape. The words for the song are on page 73.

Memory game

Can you remember the names of these things in French?
Say them out loud.
Now listen to the tape again.
Matthieu and Marion would like these for their birthday.

Des cadeaux

Birthday presents. Fit these jigsaw pieces together, and you'll find out what the other children on tape would like for their birthday.

je voudrais . . . I'd like . . .
qu'est-ce que tu veux? what do you want?
beaucoup de lots of
l'anniversaire birthday

Pairs game

Make 24 simple cards – two for each of these pictures.

 un chat
 un chien
 des bonbons
 un VTT
 une auto
 un ballon

 une radio
 des livres
 des feutres
 une corde à sauter
 une poupée
 beaucoup de cadeaux

You'll need a partner.
Deal out the cards – 12 each.
The aim is to collect pairs, so lay down any pairs you have
at the start.

1 *Player 1:* ask for a card to join to one of yours to make a pair.
   For example, if you have one dog, ask for another.
   Say, **"je voudrais un chien."**
2 Then it's *Player 2's* turn to do the same.
3 The first to lay down all the cards wins.

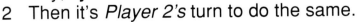

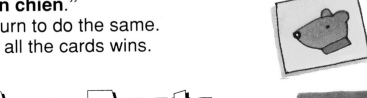

Fun Facts

Try this typical French game at your next party …
you'll recognize it, I'm sure!
Colin-maillard
You be "it." Cover your eyes and count out loud to
20 – in French, of course. Everyone else will go off
and hide.
When you get to 20, call out, **"Prêt? J'y vais!"**
(Ready? I'm coming!) and start hunting.
As you find each one, touch them and say ,
"touché" (touched, meaning "got you.")

Party quiz game

It's more fun to play this game with a partner, but you can play on your own too.

You'll need a die and markers.

1. Take turns throwing the die and move your marker along the board.
2. The first to reach the cake wins – but on the way, you must follow the instructions, out loud in French!
3. You miss a turn if you can't answer.

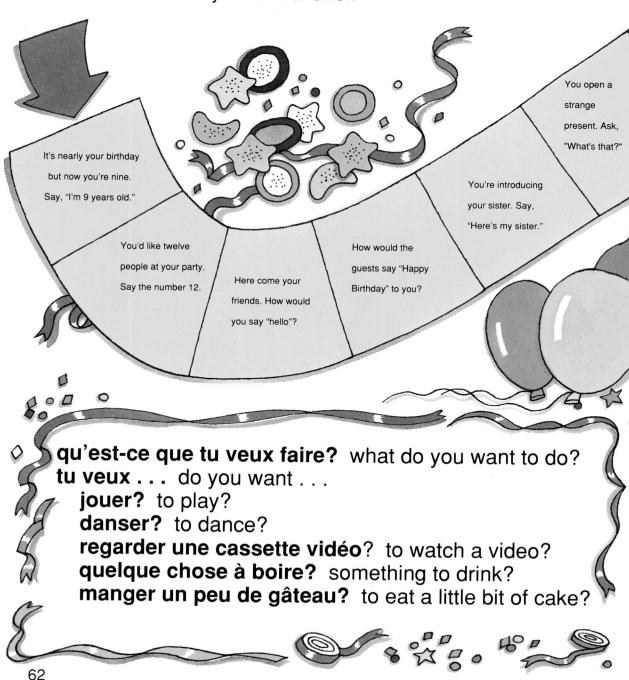

It's nearly your birthday but now you're nine. Say, "I'm 9 years old."

You'd like twelve people at your party. Say the number 12.

Here come your friends. How would you say "hello"?

How would the guests say "Happy Birthday" to you?

You're introducing your sister. Say, "Here's my sister."

You open a strange present. Ask, "What's that?"

qu'est-ce que tu veux faire? what do you want to do?
tu veux . . . do you want . . .
   jouer? to play?
   danser? to dance?
   regarder une cassette vidéo? to watch a video?
   quelque chose à boire? something to drink?
   manger un peu de gâteau? to eat a little bit of cake?

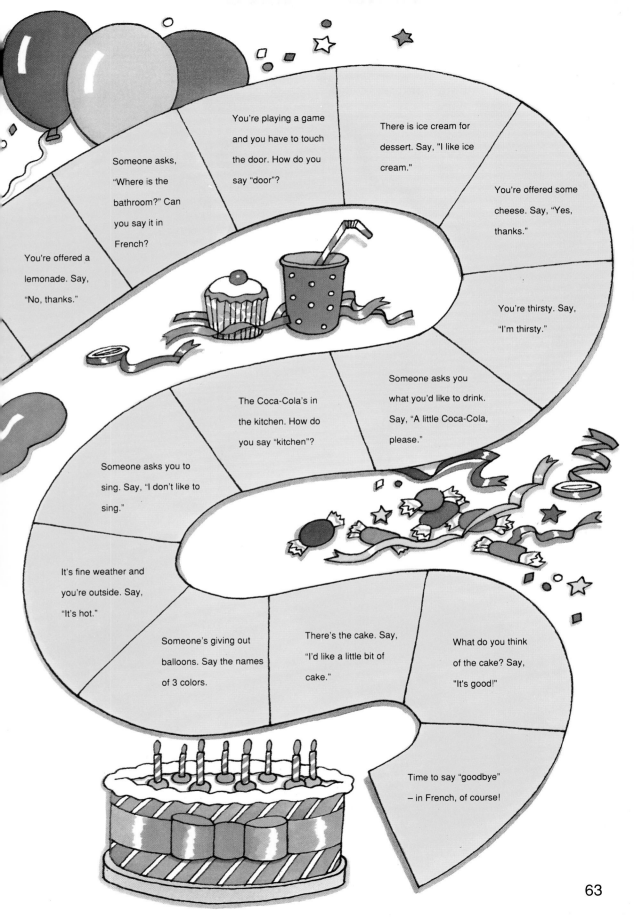

Someone asks, "Where is the bathroom?" Can you say it in French?

You're playing a game and you have to touch the door. How do you say "door"?

There is ice cream for dessert. Say, "I like ice cream."

You're offered some cheese. Say, "Yes, thanks."

You're offered a lemonade. Say, "No, thanks."

You're thirsty. Say, "I'm thirsty."

The Coca-Cola's in the kitchen. How do you say "kitchen"?

Someone asks you what you'd like to drink. Say, "A little Coca-Cola, please."

Someone asks you to sing. Say, "I don't like to sing."

It's fine weather and you're outside. Say, "It's hot."

Someone's giving out balloons. Say the names of 3 colors.

There's the cake. Say, "I'd like a little bit of cake."

What do you think of the cake? Say, "It's good!"

Time to say "goodbye" – in French, of course!

Checklist

Let's go over what you have learned in this unit. When you are sure you know what these mean, put a ✔ in the box.

- [ ] **qu'est-ce que tu veux?**

- [ ] **je voudrais . . .**

- [ ] **un chien**   **une poupée**
  un VTT   **un gâteau**   **une corde à sauter**
  des livres   **des feutres**   **beaucoup de cadeaux**

- [ ] **qu'est-ce que tu veux faire?**

- [ ] **tu veux . . .**
       danser?   **regarder une cassette vidéo?**
       jouer?   **quelque chose à boire?**

- [ ] **joyeux anniversaire!**

64

More about French

Learning a language is like breaking a code or recognizing patterns.
Did you notice some patterns in the French you have just learned?
Have a look at these:

The words for "the"

There are three words for "the" in French:

- **le** and **la**

le chat   the cat
la maison   the house

- and **les** when there is more than one thing:

les chats   the cats
les maisons   the houses

Le and **la** both shorten to **l'** in front of a vowel (a, e, i, o and u):

l'éléphant   the elephant

The words for "a"

There are two words for "a" in French:

- **un** and **une**

un chat   a cat
une maison   a house

Can you spot the pattern?
If you use **le** for "the," you use **un** for "a."
And if you use **la** for "the," you use **une** for "a."

The **le/un** words are called *masculine*.
The **la/une** words are called *feminine*.
All nouns (objects, people, and places) in French are either masculine or feminine.

As you would expect, the words for "man" and "boy" are masculine, and the words for "woman" and "girl" are feminine. Look at these examples:

un homme	a man	**une femme**	a woman
un garçon	a boy	**une fille**	a girl
un père	a father	**une mère**	a mother
un oncle	an uncle	**une tante**	an aunt
un maître	a man teacher	**une maîtresse**	a woman teacher

For most nouns though, there's no easy way of telling whether you should use **le** or **la** or **un** or **une** – you just have to learn each word! Don't panic, after a while you can *hear* if you've got it right . . . and people will still understand you, even if you get it wrong.

More than one thing

Look at this pattern:

maison house
maisons houses

chat cat
chats cats

cadeau present
cadeaux presents

gâteau cake
gâteaux cakes

So, in French, in the *plural* (when you have more than one of something), you either:
• add an "s" for most nouns, like **maisons** and **chats**
• or an "x" for nouns ending in "eau," like **cadeaux** and **gâteaux**.
But, remember you can't *hear* the "s" and "x" in French.

Try to say those words out loud. If you can't remember how to pronounce them, listen to your cassettes again.

No, not

You know how to say:

j'aime chanter   I like to sing
je n'aime pas chanter I don't like to sing

And look at:

j'ai soif   I'm thirsty
je n'ai pas soif I'm not thirsty

Can you see the pattern?
In French, to change to the *negative* (saying "no" or "not"),
you use **ne . . . pas** (**n'** is short for **ne** before a vowel).

Look at these:

j'aime la glace I like ice cream
il fait chaud   it's hot
j'ai faim   I'm hungry
je veux le bleu I want the blue one

How would you say these in French?

I do *not* like ice cream
it's *not* hot
I'm *not* hungry
I do *not* want the blue one

The answers are upside down at the foot of the page.

As you get better at French, keep trying to break the code and discover
more patterns. Soon you'll be able to make up your own sentences.
(There are lots of patterns to discover in the numbers on the next page!)

---

je ne veux pas le bleu   il ne fait pas chaud
je n'ai pas faim   je n'aime pas la glace

Answers

Numbers 1 to 1000

1	un		60	soixante
2	deux		61	soixante et un
3	trois		62	soixante-deux
4	quatre		63	soixante-trois

on with the same pattern to . . . 69, but be careful of . . .

5	cinq
6	six
7	sept
8	huit
9	neuf
10	dix

70	soixante-dix
71	soixante et onze
72	soixante-douze
73	soixante-treize
74	soixante-quatorze
75	soixante-quinze
76	soixante-seize
77	soixante-dix-sept
78	soixante-dix-huit
79	soixante-dix-neuf

11	onze
12	douze
13	treize
14	quatorze
15	quinze
16	seize
17	dix-sept
18	dix-huit
19	dix-neuf
20	vingt

80	quatre-vingts
81	quatre-vingt-un
82	quatre-vingt-deux
83	quatre-vingt-trois

now follow the usual pattern to . . . 89, but be careful again of . . .

21	vingt et un
22	vingt-deux
23	vingt-trois
24	vingt-quatre
25	vingt-cinq
26	vingt-six
27	vingt-sept
28	vingt-huit
29	vingt-neuf

90	quatre-vingt-dix
91	quatre-vingt-onze
92	quatre-vingt-douze
93	quatre-vingt-treize
94	quatre-vingt-quatorze
95	quatre-vingt-quinze
96	quatre-vingt-seize
97	quatre-vingt-dix-sept
98	quatre-vingt-dix-huit
99	quatre-vingt-dix-neuf

30	trente
31	trente et un
32	trente-deux

with the same pattern as 20 . . . to 39

40	quarante
41	quarante et un
42	quarante-deux

and on with the same pattern to . . . 49

50	cinquante
51	cinquante et un
52	cinquante-deux

and then the same pattern to . . . 59

100	cent
200	deux cents
300	trois cents
400	quatre cents
500	cinq cents
600	six cents
700	sept cents
800	huit cents
900	neuf cents
1000	mille

Songs

Unit 1

Bonjour, je m'appelle Michel.
Comment t'appelles-tu?
Bonjour, je m'appelle Michel.
Comment t'appelles-tu?

Je m'appelle Michel,
Et, salut.

Bonjour, je m'appelle Rachel.
Comment t'appelles-tu?
Bonjour, je m'appelle Rachel.
Comment t'appelles-tu?

Je m'appelle Rachel,
Et, salut.

Salut!

et = and

Un, deux, trois,
Quatre, cinq, six,
Sept, huit, neuf,
Dix.

Un, deux, trois,
Quatre, cinq, six,
Sept, huit, neuf,
Dix.

Un, deux, trois, quatre,
Cinq, six, sept, huit,
Neuf . . . dix.

Unit 2

Tu aimes le Coca?
Non.
Tu aimes la limonade?
Non.
Tu aimes la glace?
Non.
Tu aimes les fraises?
Non.
Tu aimes les pizzas?
Oui.
Seulement les pizzas?
Oui.

Tu aimes le Coca?
Non.
Tu aimes la limonade?
Non.
Tu aimes la glace?
Non.
Tu aimes les fraises?
Non.
Tu aimes les pizzas?
Oui.
Seulement les pizzas?
Oui.

seulement = only

Unit 3

J'aime l'école, j'aime l'école,
Un, deux, trois, quatre.
J'aime l'école, j'aime l'école
Un, deux, trois.

J'aime l'école, j'aime l'école,
Cinq, six, sept, huit, neuf.
J'aime l'école, j'aime l'école
Huit, neuf, dix.

Où est la salle de classe?
Où est la cour?
Où est la salle de classe?
Où est la cour?

J'aime l'école, j'aime l'école,
Un, deux, trois, quatre.
J'aime l'école, j'aime l'école.
Au revoir.

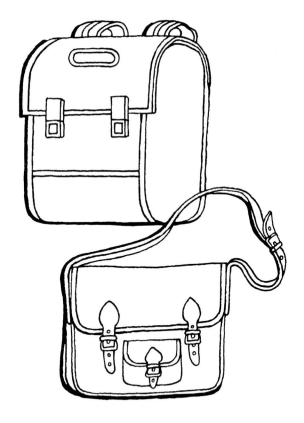

Unit 4

Voici ma famille.
Voici ma famille.
Voici Maman, voici Papa.
Voici ma famille.
J'ai deux frères
Et j'ai trois sœurs,
Et voici ma famille.

Voici ma famille.
Voici ma famille.
Voici Mamie, voici Papi.
Voici ma famille.
J'ai deux frères
Et j'ai trois sœurs,
Et voilà ma famille.
Voilà ma famille.
Voilà ma famille.

voilà = there is

Unit 5

Qu'est-ce que c'est?
Qu'est-ce que c'est?
C'est une sorcière.

Qu'est-ce que c'est?
Qu'est-ce que c'est?
C'est une sorcière.

Où est la sorcière?
Elle est ici.
Où est la sorcière?
Dans la cuisine.

Où est la sorcière?
Maintenant?
Où est la sorcière?
Dans le salon.

Qu'est-ce que c'est?
Qu'est-ce que c'est?
C'est une sorcière.

Qu'est-ce que c'est?
Qu'est-ce que c'est?
C'est une sorcière.

Où est la sorcière?
Elle est ici.
Où est la sorcière?
Dans la cuisine.

Où est la sorcière?
Maintenant?
Où est la sorcière?
Dans le salon.

elle = she
dans = in
maintenant = now

Unit 6

Je n'aime pas manger.
Je n'aime pas lire.
Je n'aime pas chanter.
J'aime dormir!

Je n'aime pas écouter
La radio.
Je n'aime pas voyager.
Non,
J'aime dormir.

Je n'aime pas manger.
Je n'aime pas lire.
Je n'aime pas chanter.
J'aime dormir!

Je n'aime pas écouter
La radio.
Je n'aime pas voyager.
Non,
J'aime dormir.

Seulement dormir!

seulement = only

71

Unit 7

Noir
Blanc
Rouge
Jaune
Bleu

Noir
Blanc
Rouge
Jaune
Bleu

Rouge et bleu font violet.
Bleu et jaune font vert.
Jaune et rouge font orange.

Noir
Blanc
Rouge
Jaune
Bleu

Noir
Blanc
Rouge
Jaune
Bleu

Noir
Blanc
Rouge
Jaune
Bleu

font = make

Unit 8

Allons visiter le zoo.
Allons voir les animaux.
Voir les lions, voir les singes,
Éléphants, girafes, chameaux.

Allons visiter le zoo.
Allons voir les animaux.
Voir les lions, voir les singes,
Éléphants, girafes, chameaux.

Ah, c'est chouette!
Ah, c'est extra!
Ah, c'est amusant!
Qu'est-ce que c'est que ça?
Ça va? Oui, ça va!

Allons visiter le zoo.
Allons voir les animaux.
Voir les lions, voir les singes,
Éléphants, girafes, chameaux.

Allons visiter le zoo.
Allons voir les animaux.
Voir les lions, voir les singes,
Éléphants, girafes, chameaux.

Allons visiter le zoo.
Allons voir les animaux.
Voir les lions, voir les singes,
Éléphants, girafes, chameaux.

visiter = visit
voir = see
chameaux = camels
qu'est-ce que c'est que ça? =
what's that?

Unit 9

Il fait beau,
Il fait chaud,
Aujourd'hui.
Un pique-nique, miam, miam,
Merci.

Il fait beau,
Il fait chaud,
Aujourd'hui.
Un pique-nique, miam, miam,
Merci.

Mais non, mais non!
Il pleut maintenant,
Et il fait froid,
Ici.

Ah voilà!

Il fait beau,
Il fait chaud,
Aujourd'hui.
Un pique-nique, miam, miam,
Bon appétit!

aujourd'hui = today
mais = but
maintenant = now

Unit 10

C'est ton anniversaire.
C'est ton anniversaire.
Tu veux jouer,
Tu veux danser?
Qu'est-ce que tu veux faire?

C'est ton anniversaire.
C'est ton anniversaire.
Tu veux manger,
Tu veux chanter?
Qu'est-ce que tu veux faire?

Voici un cadeau.
C'est un petit chien.
Voici un cadeau.
Il s'appelle Julien.

C'est ton anniversaire.
C'est ton anniversaire.
Tu veux jouer,
Tu veux danser?
Qu'est-ce que tu veux faire?
Qu'est-ce que tu veux faire?
Qu'est-ce que tu veux faire?

ton = your
il s'appelle = his name is

Word list

All the French nouns are listed with **le** or **la**.
If they start with a vowel (a, e, i, o, or u) they have **l'**, and **un** or **une** is added in parentheses.

French–English

A

à to, at

âge age;
  quel âge as-tu? how old are you?

j'ai I have

aimer to like;
  j'aime I like;
  tu aimes? do you like?

aller to go;
  allons-y!, **on y va!** let's go! come on!

amusant fun

l'an (un) year;
  j'ai . . . ans I'm . . . (years old)

l'animal (un) animal

l'anniversaire (un) birthday

appeler to call;
  comment t'appelles-tu? what's your name?
  je m'appelle my name is

après after

l'araignée (une) spider

arrête! stop!

(tu) as you have

au to the

aujourd'hui today

au revoir goodbye

aussi also, too, as well

l'auto (une) car;
  en auto in the car

aux to the

B

la baguette loaf of French bread

le ballon balloon

la banane banana

la banque bank

beau: il fait beau (*weather*) it's fine

beaucoup a lot, lots

bien good

à bientôt see you soon

blanc white

bleu blue

bon (*food*) good

bon appétit! enjoy your meal!

le bonbon candy

bon courage! good luck!

bonjour hello, good morning, good day

bravo! well done!

C

ça that;
  ça va? OK?;
  ça va OK, it's fine, I'm fine

le cadeau present

le Cameroun Cameroon

le Canada Canada

le cartable à dos backpack for school

la cassette vidéo videocassette

la chaise chair

la chambre bedroom

le chameau camel

chanter to sing

le chat cat

chaud hot;
  il fait chaud (*weather*) it's hot

le chien dog

le chocolat chocolate

chouette! super!

cinq five

le Coca Coca-Cola

combien? how much?

comment? what?;
  comment t'appelles-tu? what's your name?

comptons! let's count!

le/la concierge janitor

les copains friends

la corde à sauter jump rope

la couleur color;
  de quelle couleur? what color?

la cour playground

le couscous North African food

le couscousier pot for cooking couscous

le crayon pencil

la crêpe pancake;
  la crêperie pancake house

le croissant crescent-shaped sweet roll

la cuisine kitchen

D

dans in

danser to dance

le dauphin dolphin

de of; some, any

le dessin animé cartoon

deux two

dix ten

dix-huit eighteen

dix-neuf nineteen

dix-sept seventeen

dormir to sleep

douze twelve

E

l'eau (une) water

l'école (une) school;

l'école primaire (une) elementary school

écoute! listen!

l'éléphant (un) elephant

elle she

encore again, once more

ensemble together

est is;
  c'est it is

et and

extra! great!

F

faim: j'ai faim I'm hungry

faire to do; to make;
  ça fait that makes;
  il fait chaud *(weather)* it's hot;
  font make

la famille family

la femme wife, woman

la fête foraine amusement park

le feutre felt-tip pen

la fille girl, daughter

la fin *(race)* end

fini finished

la fraise strawberry

le franc franc

le frère brother

le frigo fridge

les frites french fries

froid cold;
  il fait froid *(weather)* it's cold

le fromage cheese

G

le galet pebble

la galette bretonne buckwheat pancake

le garçon boy

le gâteau cake

la girafe giraffe

la glace ice cream

grand big, tall

gris gray

gros big, fat

H

l'homme (un) man

huit eight

I

ici here

il he, it

il y a there is, there are

J

jaune yellow

je, j' I

jouer to play

le jour day

joyeux happy

le jus d'orange orange juice

L

là there

le lait milk

le lavabo sink

la librairie-papeterie book and stationery store

la limonade soda pop; lemonade

le lion lion
lire to read
le lit bed
le livre book

M

ma my
Madame Mrs;
  madame madam,
  ma'am
maintenant now
mais but
la maison house
le maître *(man)* teacher
la maîtresse *(woman)*
  teacher
la maman mom
la mamie grandma
manger to eat
le Mardi Gras "Fat
  Tuesday," New Orleans
  carnival
marron brown
merci thank you, thanks
la mère mother
moi me;
  c'est à moi it's mine
mon my
Monsieur Mr;
  monsieur sir
le monstre monster
la motoneige
  snowmobile

N

ne (n') . . . pas not
neuf nine
Noël Christmas

noir black
non no

O

l'oncle (un) uncle
on y va! let's go! go
  ahead!
onze eleven
l'or gold
orange orange
où? where?;
  où est? where is?;
  où sont? where are?
oui yes

P

le pain bread
le papa dad
le papi grandpa
le papier paper
la pâtisserie cakes;
  bakery
le père father
petit small, little
peu little;
  un peu de a little bit of
peur: j'ai peur I'm
  scared, afraid
le pique-nique picnic
la pizza pizza
il pleut it's raining
la pomme apple
la porte door
la poupée doll
prêt? ready?

Q

quatorze fourteen
quatre four

quel âge as-tu? how old
  are you?
quelque some
quelque chose
  something
qu'est-ce que c'est?
  what's that?
qu'est-ce qu'il y a?
  what's the matter?
**qu'est-ce que tu aimes
  faire?** what do you like
  to do?
**qu'est-ce que tu veux
  faire?** what do you
  want to do?
quinze fifteen

R

la radio radio
le rat rat
regarder to look at; to
  watch
la religieuse nun-
  shaped cake
répète! repeat!
le réveillon big meal
  served on Christmas
  Eve
rouge red

S

le sac bag
la salade lettuce,
  salad
la salle de bains
  bathroom
la salle de classe
  classroom
le salon living room

salut! hi!

le sandwich sandwich

seize sixteen

sept seven

seulement only

s'il te plaît please

s'il vous plaît *(polite)* please

le singe monkey

six six

la sœur sister

soif: j'ai soif I'm thirsty

le soleil sun; **au soleil** in the sun

sont are

la sorcière witch

le steak-frites steak and french fries

suis am

T

ta your

la table table

la tante aunt

la tartelette little tart

la télé TV, television

toi you; **à toi** your turn

les toilettes bathroom

la tomate tomato

ton your

la tourtière Canadian meat pie

tout all, everything

le train train

TGV = Train à Grande Vitesse "train of great speed," high-speed train

le traversin round pillow

treize thirteen

très very

trois three

tu you

U

un a, one

une a, one

V

va goes

vas-y! go ahead! off you go!

le vélo bike

le verre glass; **un verre de** a glass of

vert green

(je) veux I want

(tu) veux? do you want?

vingt twenty

violet purple

visiter to visit

voici here is, here are

voilà there is, there you are

voir to see

le volet shutter

le voleur thief

(je) voudrais I'd like

le voyage trip; **en voyage** on a trip

voyager to travel

le VTT mountain bike

Z

le zoo zoo

English—French

A

a un, une

after après

again encore

all tout

also aussi

amusement park la fête foraine

and et

animal l'animal (un)

apple la pomme

are sont

as well aussi

at à

aunt la tante

B

bag le sac

bakery la pâtisserie

balloon le ballon

banana la banane

bank la banque

bathroom la salle de bains; les toilettes

bed le lit

bedroom la chambre

big grand; gros

bike le vélo

birthday l'anniversaire (un)

black noir

blue bleu

book le livre; **book and stationery store** la librairie-papeterie

boy le garçon

bread le pain
brother le frère
brown marron
but mais

C

cake le gâteau
camel le chameau
candy le bonbon
car l'auto (une);
   in the car en auto
cartoon le dessin
   animé
cat le chat
chair la chaise
cheese le fromage
chocolate le chocolat
Christmas Noël
classroom la salle de
   classe
Coca-Cola le Coca
cold froid;
   it's cold (weather) il
   fait froid
color la couleur
   what color? de quelle
   couleur?
to count compter;
   let's count!
   comptons!

D

dad le papa
to dance danser
daughter la fille
day le jour
to do faire
dog le chien

doll la poupée
dolphin le dauphin
door la porte
to drink boire

E

to eat manger
eight huit
eighteen dix-huit
elephant l'éléphant (un)
eleven onze
end (race) la fin
enjoy your meal bon
   appétit!
everything tout

F

family la famille
fat gros
father le père
felt-tip pen le feutre
fifteen quinze
fine (weather) beau, il
   fait beau;
   I'm fine, it's fine
   ça va
finished fini
five cinq
four quatre
franc le franc
french fries les frites
fridge le frigo
friends les copains
fun amusant

G

giraffe la girafe
girl la fille
glass le verre;

   a glass of un verre de
to go aller;
   go ahead! vas-y!;
   let's go! allons!
   on y va!
gold l'or
good bien; (food) bon
goodbye au revoir
good luck! bon
   courage!
good morning/day
   bonjour
grandma la mamie
grandpa le papi
gray gris
great extra
green vert

H

happy joyeux;
   happy birthday!
   joyeux anniversaire!
(I) have j'ai
(you) have tu as
he il
hello bonjour
here ici;
   here is, **here are** voici
hi! salut!
hot chaud;
   it's hot (weather) il
   fait chaud
house la maison
how much is that? ça
   fait combien?
how old are you? quel
   âge as-tu?
hungry: I'm hungry j'ai
   faim

I

I je, j'
ice cream la glace
in dans
is est; *(weather)* fait;
  it is c'est, *(weather)* il
  fait
it il

J

jump rope la corde à
  sauter

K

kitchen la cuisine

L

lemonade la limonade
lettuce la salade
to like aimer;
  I like j'aime;
  do you like? tu
  aimes?
lion le lion
to listen écouter;
  listen! écoute!
little petit;
  a little bit of un peu
  de
living room le salon
to look at regarder
lots, a lot beaucoup

M

madam madame
to make faire
man l'homme (un)
me moi
milk le lait

(it's) mine c'est à moi
mom la maman
monkey le singe
monster le monstre
mother la mère
mountain bike le VTT
Mr. Monsieur
Mrs. Madame
my ma, mon;
  my name is je
  m'appelle

N

nine neuf
nineteen dix-neuf
no non
not ne (n') . . . pas
now maintenant

O

of de
off you go! allez!
OK?, are you OK? ça
  va?;
  I'm OK ça va
one un, une;
  **one more time, once
  more** encore
only seulement
orange orange
orange juice le jus
  d'orange

P

paper le papier
pebble le galet
pencil le crayon
picnic le pique-nique
pizza la pizza

to play jouer
playground la cour
please *(polite)* s'il vous
  plaît; s'il te plaît
present le cadeau
purple violet

R

radio la radio
it is raining il pleut
rat le rat
to read lire
ready? prêt?
red rouge
refrigerator le frigo
repeat! répète!

S

salad la salade
sandwich le sandwich
(I'm) scared j'ai peur
school l'école (une);
  elementary school
  l'école primaire;
  at school à l'école
scissors les ciseaux
to see voir;
  see you soon! à
  bientôt!
seven sept
seventeen dix-sept
she elle
to sing chanter
sink le lavabo
sir monsieur
sister la sœur
six six
sixteen seize
to sleep dormir

small petit

soda pop la limonade

something quelque chose

spider l'araignée (une)

steak and french fries le steak-frites

stop! arrête!

strawberry la fraise

sun le soleil;
  in the sun au soleil

super! chouette!

T

table la table

teacher *(man)* le maître, *(woman)* la maîtresse

television, TV la télé

ten dix

thank you merci

that ça;
  that makes ça fait

there là;
  there is, **there are** il y a;
  there is, **there you are** voilà

these are ce sont

thief le voleur

thirsty: I'm thirsty j'ai soif

thirteen treize

three trois

to à;
  to the au, aux

today aujourd'hui

together ensemble

tomato la tomate

too aussi

train le train

to travel voyager

too aussi

trip le voyage;
  on a trip en voyage

twelve douze

twenty vingt

two deux

U

uncle l'oncle (un)

V

very très

videocassette la cassette vidéo

to visit visiter

W

(I) want je veux;

(you) want tu veux

to watch regarder

water l'eau (une)

well done! bravo!

what? qu'est-ce que?

what do you like to do? qu'est-ce que tu aimes faire?

what do you want to do? qu'est-ce que tu veux faire?

what's that? qu'est-ce que c'est?;

what's the matter? qu'est-ce qu'il y a?

what's your name? comment t'appelles-tu?

where? où?;
  where is? où est?;
  where are? où sont?

which? quel?

white blanc

wife la femme

witch la sorcière

woman la femme

(I) would like je voudrais

Y

year l'an (un)

yellow jaune

yes oui

you tu, toi

your ta, ton;
  your turn à toi

Z

zoo le zoo